The Stour Valley Path

62 Miles from Newmarket to Cattawade

By Joe Jackson

© Joe Jackson, 2021
First Edition

This guide has been self published.

All maps provided are OS Opendata with additions . It is strongly recommended to take a detailed up-to-date map of the area with you. The route is well waymarked but there are areas which may require some basic map reading skills.

For walks and video guides for hundreds of routes all over Great Britain then visit:
www.lakedistrict-walks.co.uk

Contains OS data © Crown Copyright and database right (2020) Maps created using OpenData: OS VectorMap® District, OS OpenMap Local and OS 1:250,000 Scale Colour Raster™ with additions.

While every effort is made by myself to ensure the accuracy of this guidebook before going to print, changes can occur during the lifetime of an edition. It is recommended that you check local information like public transport, shops and accommodation if any of these will be required prior to starting the trail. Even rights of way can be altered over time.

Please keep to the countryside code by being safe, plan ahead and follow any signs. Leave gates and property as you find them. Protect plants and animals by taking litter home. Keep dogs under close control and please be considerate to other people.

Front Cover: Cavendish

Contents

Route Overview 4
Route Breakdowns 6
Planning the Route 7

Stage 1: Newmarket to Kedington 8
Stage 2: Kedington to Long Melford 22
Stage 3: Long Melford to Nayland 44
Stage 4: Nayland to Cattawade 63

Appendix 77
Personal Notes 82

The Stour Valley Path
62 Miles from Newmarket to Cattawade

The Stour Valley Path is a 62 mile long waymarked trail that begins its meandering route to the coast in the small town of Newmarket. After traversing part of the catchment area of the River Stour, it largely follows the watercourse along the border of Suffolk and Essex to reach the Stour Estuary at Manningtree. The path encounters many stunning ancient sites including the Devil's Ditch Saxon Earthwork, Clare Priory and Castle ruins as well as many listed houses of Cavendish and Long Melford. The gently flowing watercourse naturally attracts lots of wildlife including many species of dragonflies and birds during the spring and summer months. Several sites including Sudbury Meadows and Cattawade Marshes really increase the varieties that can be seen with a chance to see the elusive Redshank and Oystercatcher. The final 10 miles really tops off this great route by exploring the stunning countryside that makes up the Dedham Vale Area of Outstanding Natural Beauty which is known as Constable Country after the legendary painter John Constable who took inspiration from another local painter, Thomas Gainsborough.

Recommended Maps for Route:
OS Explorer (1:25,000)
210 - Newmarket & Haverhill
196 - Sudbury, Hadleigh & Dedham Vale
197 - Ipswich, Felixstowe & Harwich

Grid References for Start and Finish
Start: TL 646 636
Finish: TM 101 332

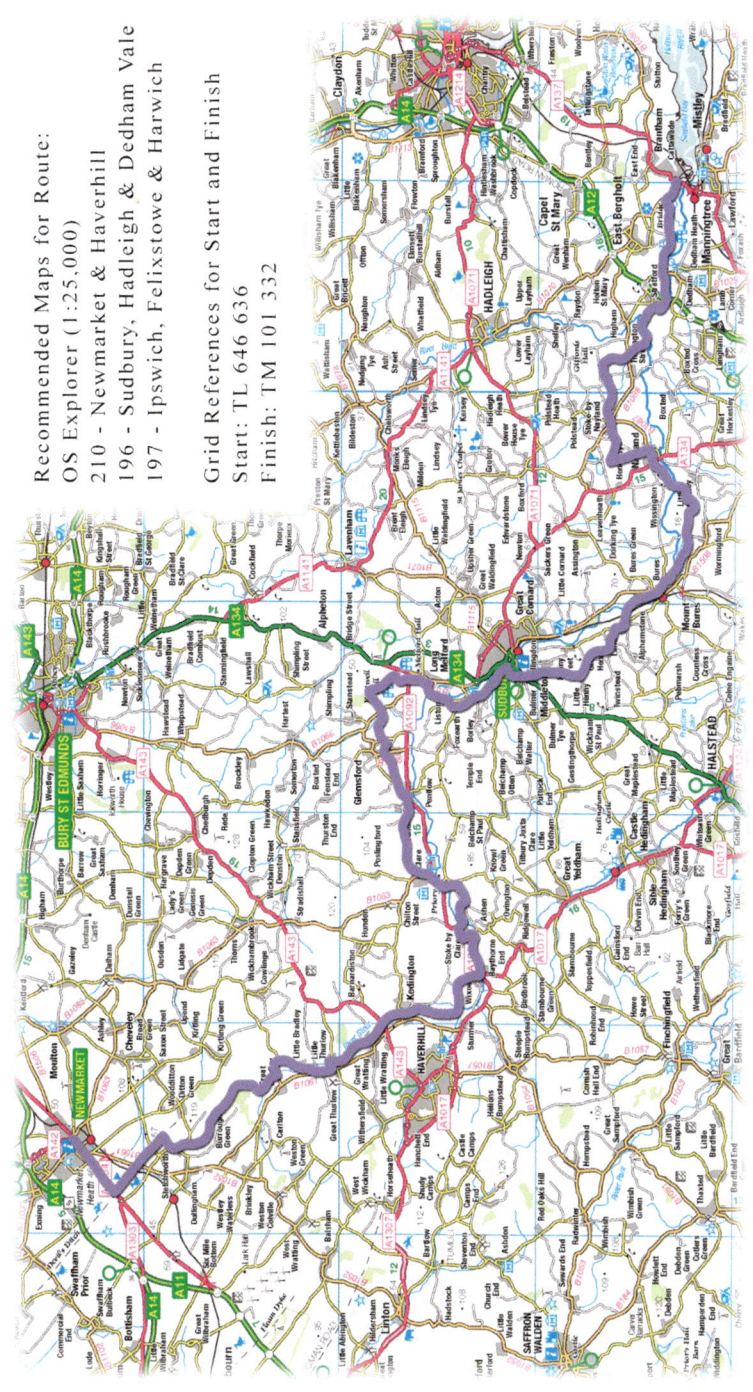

Walk Breakdown

The Stour Valley Path is fairly well served by public transport, especially beyond the village of Clare. This, along with plenty of overnight accommodation means you can break the walk down over more than four days. Here are some examples of five and seven day breakdowns.

5 Section Breakdown:

Stage 1:	Newmarket to Kedington	(25.0km / 15.5 Miles)
Stage 2:	Kedington to Clare	(13.0km / 8.07 Miles)
Stage 3:	Clare to Sudbury	(21.8km / 13.5 Miles)
Stage 4:	Sudbury to Nayland	(21.5km / 13.4 Miles)
Stage 5:	Nayland to Cattawade	(21.2km / 13.2 Miles)

7 Section Breakdown:

Stage 1:	Newmarket to Stetchworth	(8.1km / 5.03 Miles)
Stage 2:	Stetchworth to Kedington	(16.9km / 10.5 Miles)
Stage 3:	Kedington to Clare	(13.0km / 8.07 Miles)
Stage 4:	Clare to Long Melford	(15.4km / 9.56 Miles)
Stage 5:	Long Melford to Bures	(17.1km / 10.6 Miles)
Stage 6:	Bures to Stoke by Nayland	(14.8km / 9.19 Miles)
Stage 7:	Stoke by Nayland to Cattawade	(15.8km / 9.81 Miles)

Planning Your Route

Below is a list of all of the villages and towns that the route either passes through or very near to, allowing you to plan where to take rests, top up on supplies or stay overnight. If planning an overnight stay please remember to book well in advance with details on many of the local hotels and B&B's available in the appendix. **Bold** indicates the suggested end point for each stage. Although some of these may not provide overnight accommodation they all have public transport links to a nearby town with either hotels or B&Bs.

Location	Distance	Facilities
Newmarket	0.0km / 0.0 Miles	Shops, Pubs, B&B
Stetchworth	8.1km / 5.0 Miles	Pub, B&B
Little Bradley	17.5km / 10.9 Miles	None
Little Thurlow	19.1km / 11.9 Miles	Pub
Great Thurlow	19.9km / 12.4 Miles	None
Kedington	25.0km / 15.5 Miles	Shop, Pub
Baythorne End	30.5km / 18.9 Miles	None
Stoke by Clare	33.5km / 20.8 Miles	Shop, Pub, B&B
Clare	38.0km / 23.6 Miles	Shops, Pubs, B&B
Cavendish	43.1km / 26.8 Miles	Shop, Pubs, B&B
Glemsford	46.2km / 28.7 Miles	Shops, Pubs, B&B
Long Melford	53.4km / 33.2 Miles	Shops, Pubs, B&B
Sudbury	59.8km / 37.1 Miles	Shops, Pubs, B&B
Middleton	62.3km / 38.7 Miles	None
Great Henny	63.9km / 39.7 Miles	None
Lamarsh	68.2km / 42.4 Miles	Pub
Bures	70.5km / 43.8 Miles	Shop, Pub, B&B
Wormingford	74.2km / 46.1 Miles	Pub
Nayland	81.3km / 50.5 Miles	Shop, Pub, B&B
Stoke by Nayland	85.3km / 53.0 Miles	Shops, Pubs, B&B
Stratford St Mary	93.8km / 58.3 Miles	Pubs, B&B
Dedham	96.0km / 59.6 Miles	Shop, Pubs, B&B
Flatford	98.3km / 61.0 Miles	Cafe
Cattawade	101.1km / 62.8 Miles	Pub

The first stage of the Stour Valley Path begins in the Suffolk town of Newmarket and treads a route along the ancient Devil's Ditch earthwork. Several lovely small Cambridgeshire villages are passed including Stetchworth and Little Thurlow as the upper reaches of the Stour Valley are finally joined close to Great Bradley. Eventually the village of Kedington is reached where a bus can be caught into nearby Haverhill or Bury St Edmunds for an overnight stay and return the following day.

Stage 1: Newmarket to Kedington
Distance: 25.0km / 15.5 Miles

From the clocktower in the centre of Newmarket follow the high street south west past dozens of shops and numerous pubs and cafes. After about 1km the road begins to leave Newmarket and head out in a straight line with Newmarket Race Course on the right. You need to stick to the roadside pavement for a further 2.3km in a straight line south west until you reach the large sign for entering Cambridgeshire. On the left is a public footpath which follows the line of the ancient earthwork known as the Devil's Ditch through the trees and to open countryside. The route follows the top of the ancient earthwork for just over 1 mile (1.6km) to the south east eventually crossing the railway line and ending up at a road. Cross carefully and join the path on the opposite side which sticks to the top of the ancient earthwork through narrow woodland and after 1.2km the path will arrive at another road.

Newmarket

Newmarket is a small town on the edge of Suffolk and considered the birthplace of thoroughbred horse racing. Up to one in three jobs in the town relate to horse racing, not surprising when you realise its the largest racehorse training centre in Britain. The busy high street is home to dozens of chain and independent shops and cafes making it the perfect pace to start a long distance trail with excellent public transport links via bus and train.

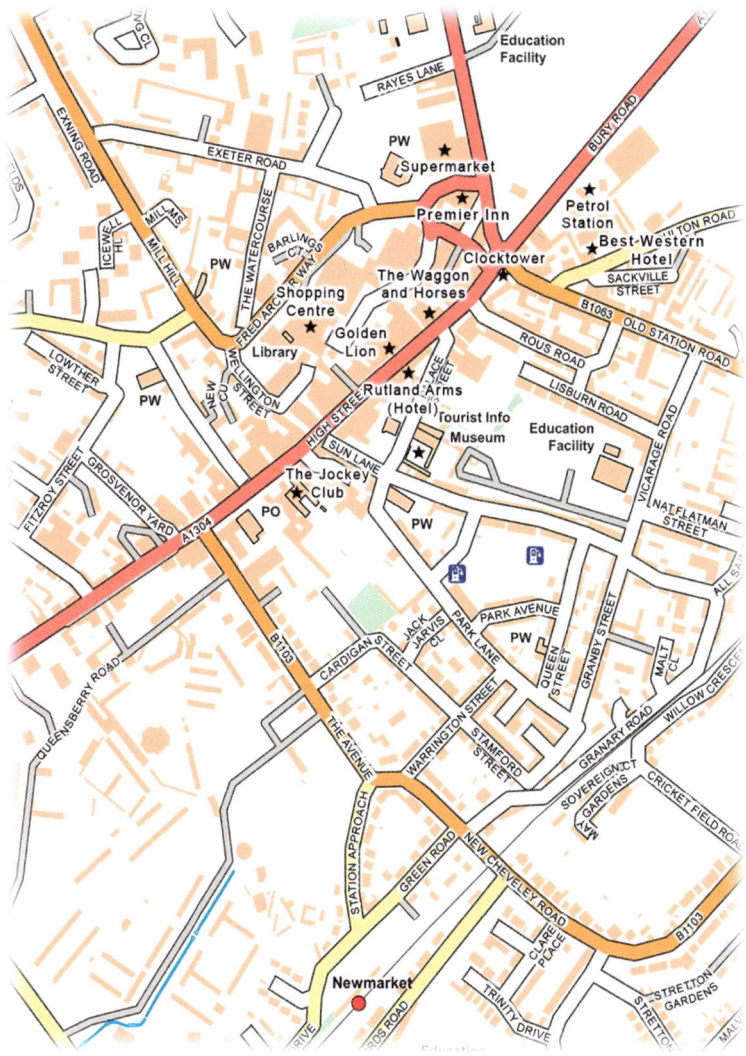

The Clocktower

The clock tower in the centre of Newmarket dates to 1887 and was erected to commemorate Queen Victoria's Golden Jubilee. The tower is protected as a Grade II listed building and officially marks the start of the Stour Valley Path.

Newmarket Clocktower

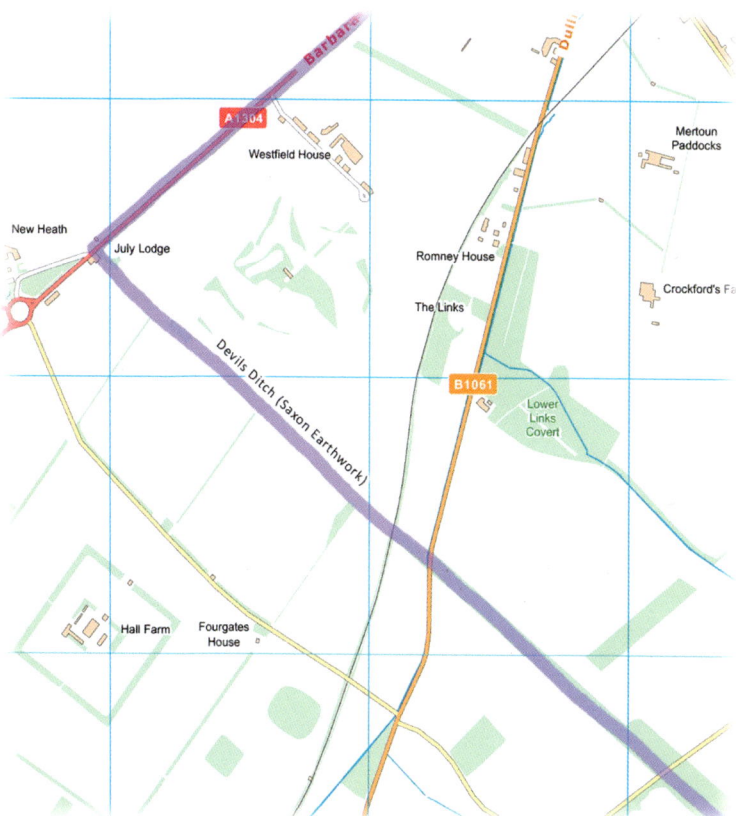

Cross the road carefully and follow the path up the steps onto the earthwork opposite signposted to Wooditton. The earthwork path is followed south east for 1km to a split in the path which also marks the point where the Icknield Way Trail is joined. Turn right and follow the path along the field edge to the south west and after about 750m the path follows a narrow alley, crosses a road and down another narrow hedge-lined path to the main road through the village of Stetchworth. Turn left and follow the road for about 350m to a public footpath on the right through a gate. The path follows the edge of the horse paddock and continues straight ahead at the track. The path continues south along the paddock to a horse riding track. Cross the track at the crossing and follow the path towards the woodland up ahead and bears right along the edge of the wood to a trackway by a footbridge. The track along the edge of Marmers Wood is followed south east (ignore the path branching off right along the Icknield Way Trail) for just over 200m when the wood is left and continues up to the edge of Basefield Wood just ahead.

The Devil's Ditch

The enormous earthwork known as the Devil's Ditch or Devil's Dyke is an 11km long bank and ditch that at its highest point reaches 34ft over the surrounding chalk grassland. It is the largest of a series of earthworks that are thought to help control movement along the Icknield Way and likely built in the Anglo-Saxon period.

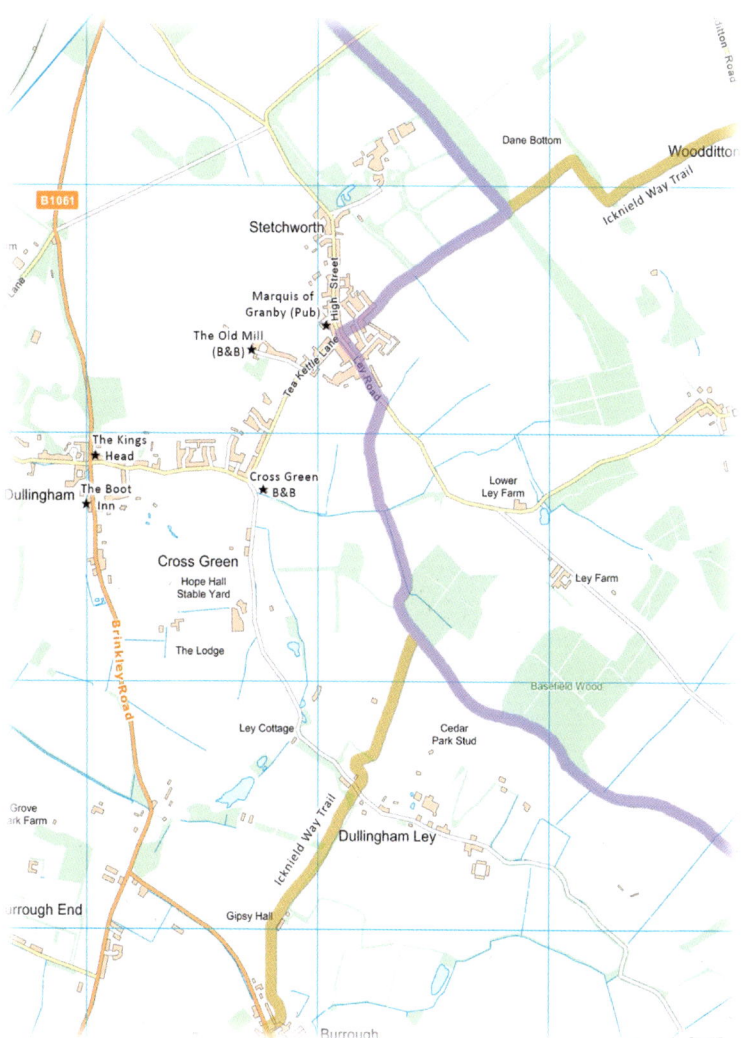

The path continues past Basefield Wood and sticks to the same path gently meandering to the south east and after 1.1km arrives at the edge of Ten Wood. The edge of Ten Wood is followed for just over 800m where the path joins the edge of the open field and heads over to the edge of Great Widgham Wood which consists of a majority of pines and evergreen trees. At the end of the wood the path heads through a small meadow and crosses a narrow stream to a track. Turn right and follow the track past a series of weirs, ignoring all paths heading off left and right, and after just over 1km the track splits in two. Bear right and follow the straight track until you reach the River Stour.

The Icknield Way

The Stour Valley Path briefly joins the Icknield Way Trail, another long distance path which begins in Buckinghamshire and ends just near Thetford in Norfolk. The route follows the general line of Britain's oldest road and links the Ridgeway to the Peddars Way, two well known ancient routes.

Icknield Way Sighpost

Cross the River Stour and follow the road ahead for just 50m to a footpath on the left. The path hugs the field edge and continues up to a small copse where the path passes along its edge and round a sharp bend left then right and along the field edge to the road. Turn left and follow the road around a sharp S-Bend and then along a straight section of road until you reach the first house on the right. Just before the house is a footpath on the right along the field edge to the south. The path follows the field edge and then crosses the next open field to a track. Here the track bends round to the left across the field and then at the other side gently bears right and heads south up to the road.

Church of All Saints, Little Bradley

Little Bradley Church is an impressive Grade I listed building dating to the mid 11th Century making it the oldest building encountered on the walk so far. It is possible that the lower section of the tower is late Saxon in origin or built soon after the Norman Conquest of 1066.

Little Bradley Church

At the road turn right and follow the lane past Little Bradley Church and over a bridge over the River Stour. Just after the bridge the Stour Valley Path turns left and follows the field edge south until it reaches the road close to Little Thurlow Church. Cross the church yard to the right and once at the track turn right and then left almost straight away along a diagonal path. Continue straight ahead at the next field and follow the path along the side of the school and up to the road. Turn left and follow the road south through Little Thurlow to The Cock Inn. About 50m past the pub is a long driveway on the left, head down here and at the woodland cross the bridge and bear right to the field edge path. The field edge is followed to a grazing field which is then passed through and at the other side the road is joined just after a small graveyard.

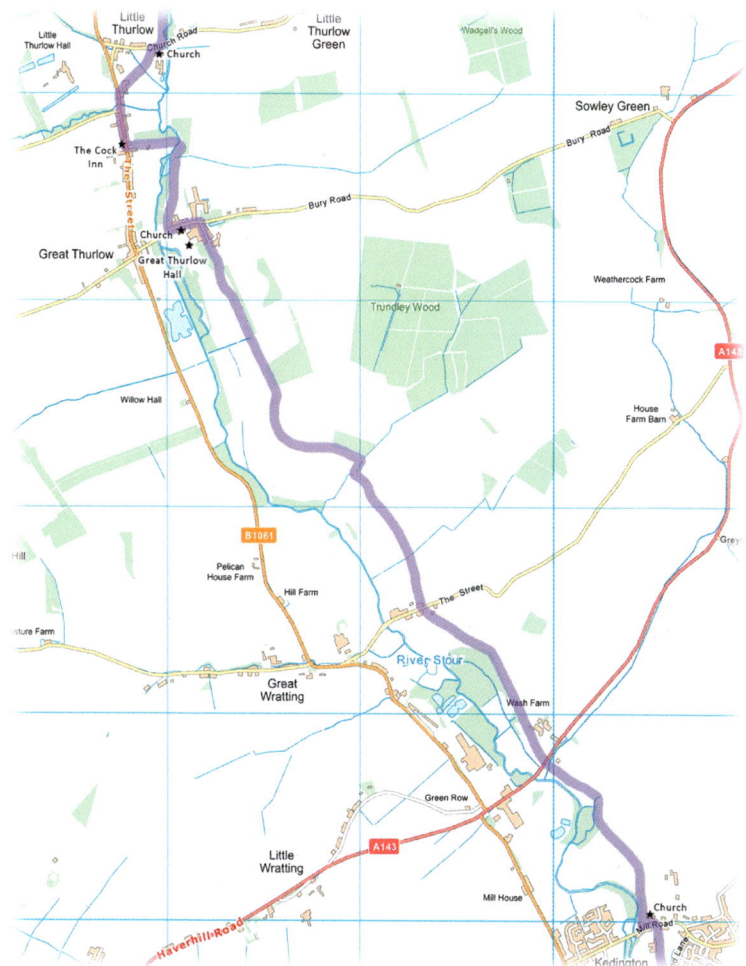

Turn left and follow the road about 50m past the church to a public right of way along a track on the right. The track heads through the farm and out the other side and up to a sharp bend just ahead. Here the route enters the grazing field on the right and sticks to the left hand edge around a small clump of trees and into the next field. Follow the left hand edge of the next field and through a third field to the far corner. Here the path exits the grazing fields onto a track and turns right and follows the edge of the field gently round to the east to join a wide trackway. The track is followed for about 200m to the edge of the wood and bends sharply right and then round to the left and eventually up to the road.

St Peter, Little Thurlow

Little Thurlow Church is dedicated to St Peter and dates to the early 14th Century. Some elements of the church date even earlier, to the 12th Century, and have either been brought here from an older church or the present structure replaced an older building.

St Peter, Little Thurlow

Opposite the path continues along the edge of a property and diagonally across the field to Lion Meadow Plantation. The path follows the left hand edge of the plantation and reaches some paddocks which are crossed and the A143 is reached. Cross the main road carefully and join the footpath opposite which follows the edge of the meadow to the open field on the other side. Bear right and follow the field edge for a short way before the path turns left and crosses the field past telegraph lines and into the church yard in Kedington. Head up to the road and turn left looking out for a long straight avenue of trees on the right opposite the entrance to the church yard. Follow the avenue of trees up to the road and turn right, sticking to the road past the convenience store and up to the Barnardiston Arms. Just round the corner from the pub is a bus stop providing services into nearby Haverhill for an overnight stay and returning the following morning.

River Stour

All Saints, Great Thurlow

The Grade II* listed church of All Saints in Great Thurlow retains some of its Norman features and underwent restorations in 1741, 1880 and 1956.

All Saints, Great Thurlow

St Peter, Kedington

Kedington Church is a large Grade I listed building dedicated to St Peter and St Paul. Some of the stonework of the church is of Norman origin and dated to circa 1140 with the main structure supposedly built on top of a Roman Villa!

The second day along the Stour Valley Path begins in the village of Kedington and immediately follows the valley floor south to Baythorne End. Here the path turns east and takes a meandering route through many stunning historic villages including Clare, with its massive Norman Motte & Bailey Castle and Cavendish with dozens of timber framed houses. At the end of the day is the stunning village of Long Melford with its two historic country houses and wide open high street filled with independent shops and cafes.

Stage 2: Kedington to Long Melford
Distance: 28.9km / 17.94 Miles

Follow the track along the left side of the Barnardiston Arms which heads south past the community centre and paddocks up to sewage works. Keep left along the edge of the sewage works continuing south which joins a path along the edge of open fields. The path is lined by trees on the left with the River Stour meandering its way along the valley floor not too far behind. Stick to the field edge path south with numerous little twists and turns and after 2km it crosses an open field to the trees on the far side. Turn left along the field edge followed by meadows up to a footbridge.

Kedington

Kedington is a lovely small village with a village pub and convenience store perfectly situated at the end of a long first days walking. Regular buses provide transport into Haverhill and Bury St Edmunds for an overnight stay as there is no overnight accommodation in the village.

Cross the River Stour via the footbridge and along the path on the other side which follows a curve around the nearby farm to join a field edge and begins an ascent up the side of the valley. As the path starts to level off it passes through some trees and then crosses two open fields to the east to join a narrow country lane. Turn right and follow the lane through Thistlely Common and up to the main road just after the old railway bridge. Turn right to follow the A1092 over the River Stour by Baythorne Mill and up to the junction just ahead. Turn left and after just 50m the Stour Valley Path turns left down the driveway for Baythorne Park. The drive is followed until a bend about 300m away where the path bears left across the grazing field and up to a large pond.

The Old Railway

Hints of the old railway line can be seen along much of the days walking from Kedington to Long Melford. The line, which once connected Marks Tey in Essex to Great Shelford in Cambridgeshire, follows the meandering River Stour along the valley floor, parts of which can be traced as raised banks and railway bridges. The line opened in 1865 but sadly closed in 1967 as part of the Beeching cuts.

Railway Bridge near Baythorne End

Baythorne Park

Part of the Stour Valley Path passes through the vast estate of Baythorne Park overlooked by the spectacular Grade II listed house. The house dates to the late 17th Century and recently sold for £11million!

Follow the path past the pond and through the small section of woodland to the field edge. The path continues along the field edge to the north east with the river only just over to the left. Once into the next field the path heads away from the river to the right. The path follows the field edge and through another small section of woodland to arrive at open grazing fields. Here the path is lost a little but heads across the field to the river along a faint track which then follows the riverbank round to a series of gates close to Stoke College and up to the road. Turn left and follow the lane north into the village of Stoke by Clare which arrives at the village shop and pub.

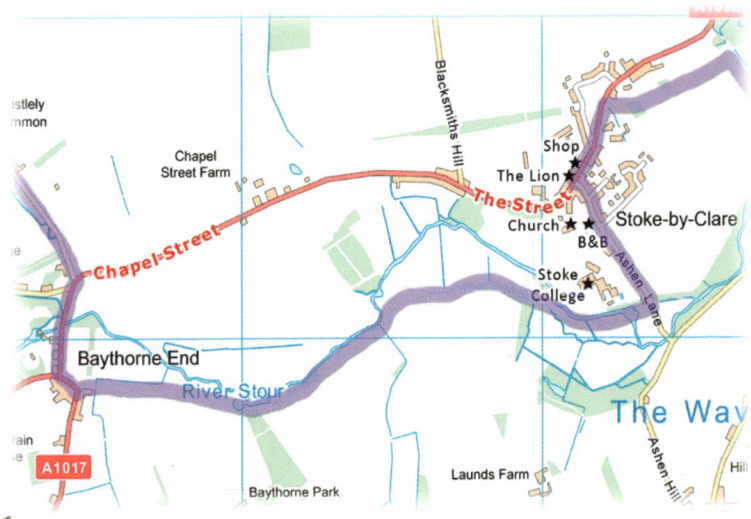

St John, Stoke by Clare

The lovely Grade I listed church of St John the Baptist sits just north of Stoke College and largely dates to the 16th Century with older buildings incorporated into the current structure. The tower dates to the 14th Century and a chapel on the south side has walls dated to the 13th Century. It is known that a Priory Church existed on the site in 1124 and is likely these older elements relate to this.

Stoke by Clare village green

Stoke College

Stoke College sits close to a bend in the River Stour on the edge of the tiny village of Stoke by Clare. The site was originally a Benedictine Convent founded in 1050 with the present day building largely dating to the 18th Century and incorporating older elements. The Grade II* listed building is now used as an independent school.

Turn right to follow the A1092 through the village for just 250m to a footpath along the old railway line on the right opposite the large village green. The path is followed for 450m to a fenced garden just before the road. If you reach the road you have gone too far as the path turns right along the edge of the garden to the south east and through a gate to cross the River Stour by a weir. Turn left along the river briefly and bear right across this field and then across the next one in a straight line past one boundary and up to a second. Cross through the tree line and follow the field edge on the left until you reach the road.

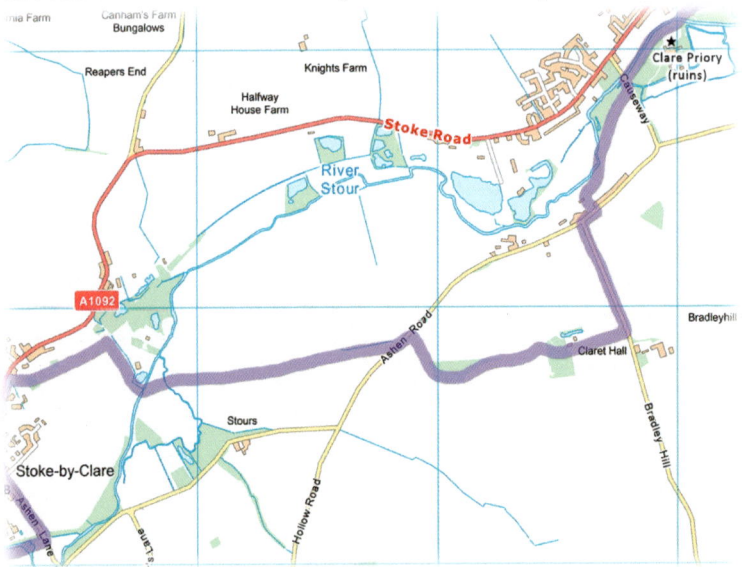

Turn left along the road and after just 70m the Stour Valley Path turns right onto a trackway which gently curves between fields and into the nearby wood. The track continues almost as far as Claret Hall but just before entering the grounds turns right through another small section of woodland round to the driveway and out up to the road. Turn left and follow the road downhill to the junction and then turn right, looking out for a footpath on the left after just 50m. The turn left feels like a trespass but the right of way does go down the driveway and along the edge of the garden before turning right just a stones throw from the river. The path then heads along the back of a series of gardens and then along a field edge to the road. Turn left and then right just before the bridge just ahead which leads along a riverside footpath surrounded by woodland and crosses the River Stour via an old railway bridge into the car park for Clare Country Park. It's just worth noting that opposite the railway bridge on the south side of the Stour is the entrance to Clare Priory, a worthy little detour!

Clare Priory

Clare Priory sits close to the banks of the River Stour on the outskirts of Clare. Founded in 1248, it was the first house of the Augustinian Friars in England and amazingly repurchased by them in 1953 providing a comfortable retreat for those of the religious house. The ruins of the church and cloister are free to explore and create a relaxing environment for a little lunch stop.

Clare Priory Ruins

Clare Castle

Clare Castle is a spectacular Norman Motte & Bailey castle by the banks of the River Stour and now converted into a lovely country park. The Motte towers over the surrounding village with part of the stone Keep remaining on the summit and curtain wall just to the east. Construction of the castle began shortly after the Norman Conquest of 1066 on the site of an Anglo-Saxon Manor House with the first documented evidence of its existence in 1090.

Clare Camp

Clare Camp, sometimes referred to as Erbury, lies just on the northern edge of the village and likely predates all other sites of historic significance in the area. Although no significant excavations have taken place within the earthworks to establish its origin, most of the evidence suggests the ramparts and ditches are prehistoric as it resembles a standard Iron Age Hillfort.

Clare Camp Earthworks

Head through the car park and into the country park, following the tarmac path through and up to the old station cafe. Another short detour would be to the top of the motte just to the north offering some amazing views over Clare and the surrounding countryside. Once at the old station cafe continue along the tarmac to the east and over a footbridge where you need to then turn left and follow the path north bearing right after about 200m which leads along the edge of a small graveyard to the main road. Turn right and after just 40m turn left along the edge of a car park for the recreation ground keeping right along the track past several buildings until you reach the end of the track. Here the path continues directly ahead into the trees and follows the edge of the woodland to arrive at the edge of a field. The path then sticks to the edge of the field up to a track close to Hermitage Farm.

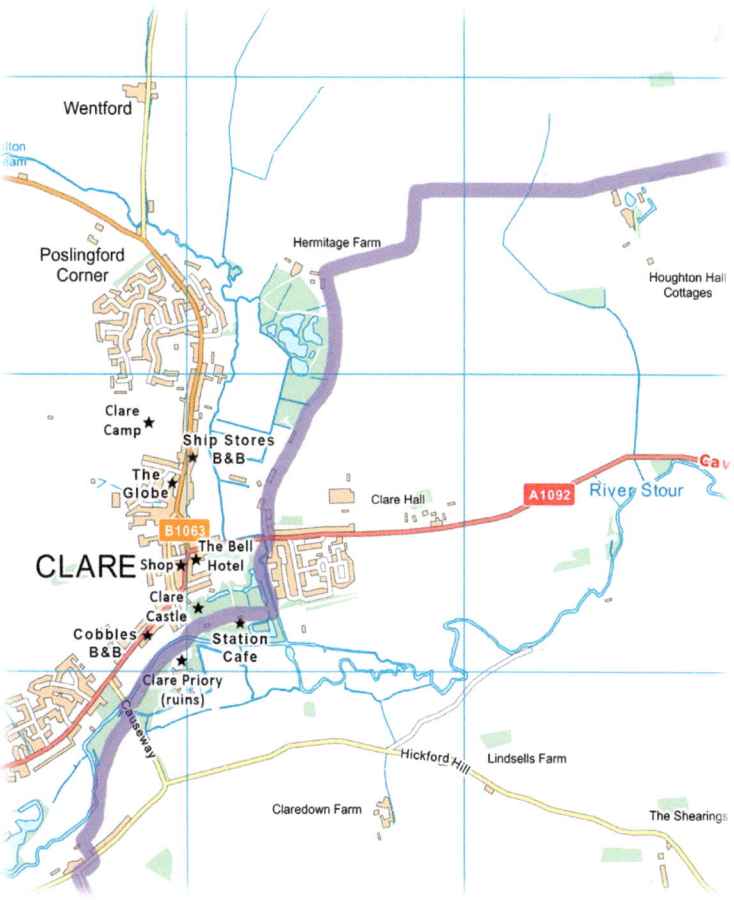

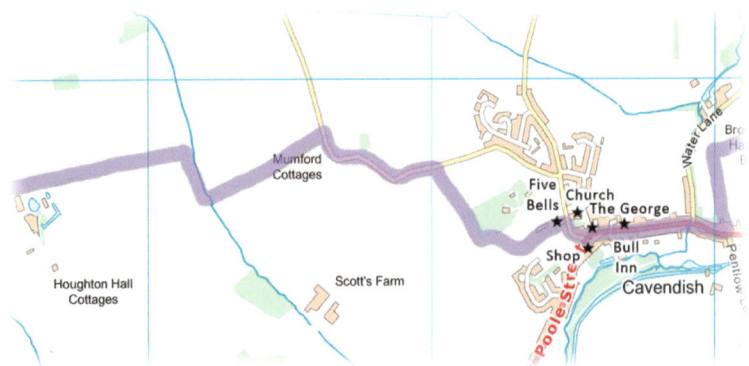

Turn right along the track which gently ascends along the edge of the field and then crosses through the tree line at the first corner. The path turns left along the field edge and round to the right before heading across the field to join a well defined track. Follow the track east for almost 300m to Houghton Hall and then an additional 200m past the hall. The path passes through the field boundary to the right and follows the field edge to rejoin the same track just ahead. The track crosses the field to the other side and turns right, following the edge for about 170m to a footpath on the left through the trees which then follows the field edge up to the road. Turn right and follow the lane around a series of bends looking out for the second footpath on the right (the first being by a sharp bend, the second about 150m further along the lane). Turn right along the field edge and after 300m turns left through the field boundary and diagonally across the small meadow. The path then passes along the edge of the graveyard to arrive at Cavendish Green.

Countryside around Clare

St Mary, Cavendish

Cavendish Church is a lovely ancient building which overlooks the iconic village green. Dedicated to St Mary, construction began in around 1300 with numerous additions through the centuries. The building is protected with a Grade I listing.

Cavendish Church behind cottages

Follow the track towards the church to the Five Bells and turn right leading to one of the most iconic scenes in the area with a picturesque view to stunning timber framed houses backed by Cavendish Church (see cover photo). Once at the main road turn left past The George and along the main street in Cavendish. Continue for just over 500m to a footpath on the left opposite Pentlow Lane (signposted to Foxearth, Pentlow and Pentlow Farm). The path passes between houses to the recreation ground and in a straight line across the field to a crop field on the other side. Continue just over 100m through the field to a crossways and turn right up to the field edge. The path passes through the boundary, briefly turns right and then left across two fields to a paddock. The path follows the edge of the paddock to the corner of the field and turns left briefly to then cross the boundary on the right and cross two fields up to a track. Follow the track straight ahead past a house and round to the left. Turn right opposite the next houses encountered along the edge of the field to the corner and then along a narrow path between properties and out of a driveway onto the road in Glemsford.

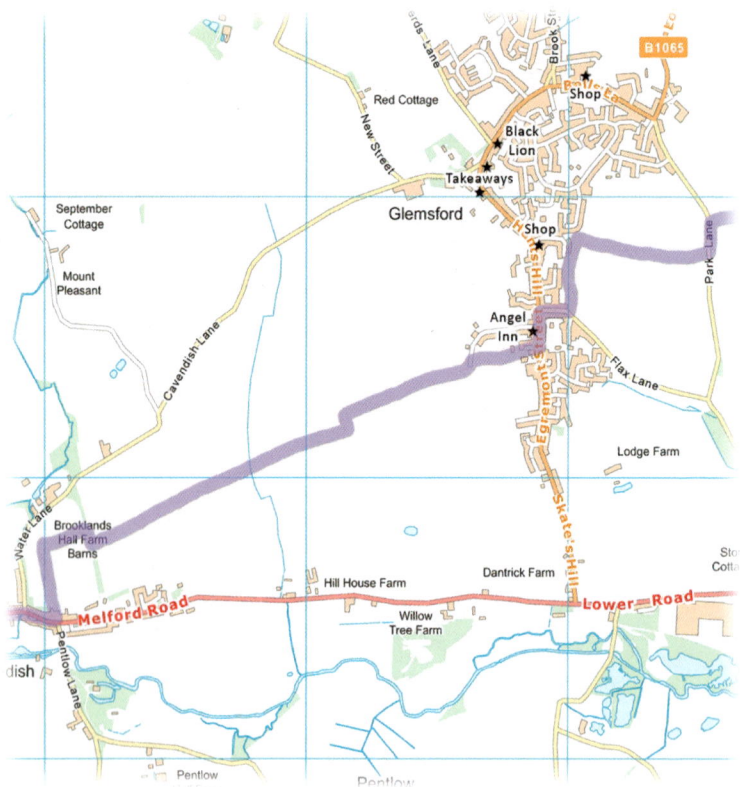

36

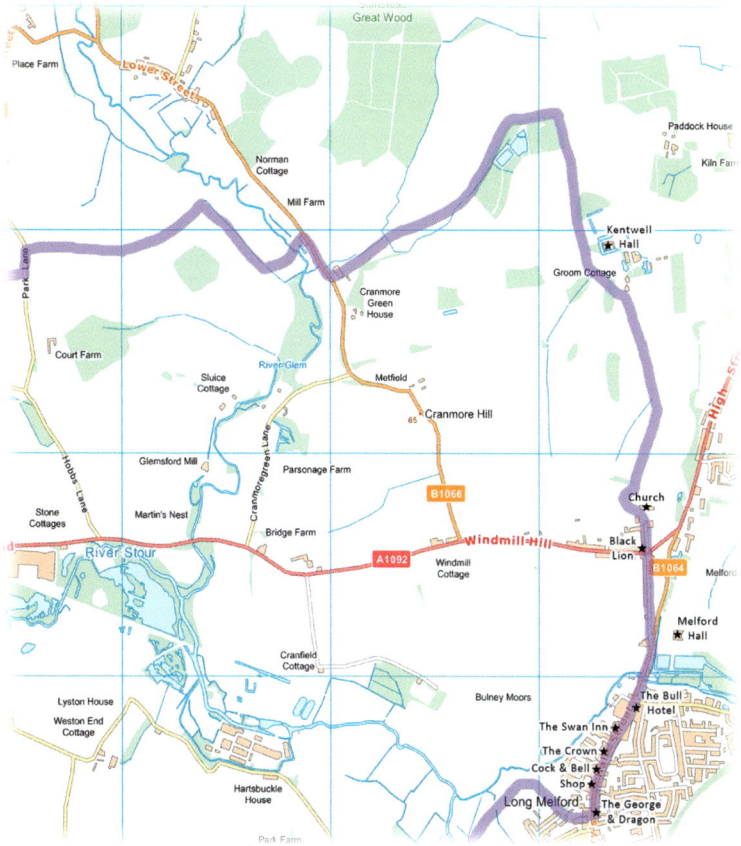

Turn left along the road for about 150m, past the Angel pub and turn right down Flax Lane. Follow the lane for just over 100m to a footpath on the left which heads along the edge of properties and after 270m arrives at a crossways. Turn right here along the edge of the field and at the far side arrives at a road. Turn left and follow the road for just 100m to a footpath on the right on the opposite side of the road. The path follows the left hand edge of three open fields to the far corner of the third and then turns right and follows the edge for a further 420m to a crossways. Turn left across the field to the River Glem and cross via the narrow footbridge to a path on the other side between properties to the road. Turn right to follow the road for 180m to Cranmore Green Farm and a footpath sign on the left. Turn left past the farm and along the left hand edge of the field behind which leads to an open field where the path crosses it diagonally to the right. The path joins the edge of the field and continues north east keeping woodlands to the right and eventually joins a track.

At the track turn right and follow it towards the wood as it passes around the trees to a split close to Kentwell Hall. Bear left at the split and head through the gate just ahead into the field and continue along the edge to the track. Turn left and follow the track through the gate and small woodland to the entrance avenue to Kentwell Hall. Turn right to follow the long line of trees along Kentwell Avenue for 500m to a footpath on the right across the grazing field. On the other side of the field the path passes through a gate and woodland to cross a small field on the other side to a track. Turn left and follow the path between paddocks and up to the spectacular Holy Trinity church. Bear right along the main walkway towards the road and follow Church Walk (lane) south to the Black Lion. Cross the road carefully and continue south along the edge of Melford Green with Melford Hall just over to the left. The footway and road crosses a narrow stream (Chad Brook) and arrives at the busy high street of Long Melford.

Gentle rolling hills around Glemsford

Kentwell Hall

Kentwell Hall is one of two absolutely stunning moated mansions seen in just a 1 mile stretch of the Stour Valley Path. This Grade I listed building dates to the 16th Century with mention of it being new in 1563 and is surrounded by a water filled moat on all sides. The house is open to the public throughout the season allowing exploration of its stunning gardens and life in Tudor times. If you're going to enjoy a rest day in Long Melford then this hall, along with Melford Hall must be on the itinerary!

Kentwell Hall

Kentwell Avenue

The base of Market Cross, Long Melford Green

Holy Trinity, Long Melford

Long Melford Church is one of the most stunning churches in Suffolk and protected as a Grade I listed building. The church largely dates to 1495 and incorporates elements of an older Norman church that once stood on the same site, itself predated by a Saxon church. It is also a fine example of a medieval wool church, founded and financed by wealthy wool merchants similar to nearby Lavenham.

Long Melford Church

Melford Hall

Melford Hall, in the management of the National Trust, dates to 1559 making it only a few years older than nearby Kentwell Hall. It incorporates parts of an older structure held by the abbots of Bury St Edmunds which was in use before the Norman Conquest. The house is also open to the public through the main season as well as some of the surrounding parkland and its ornamental gardens.

The third and penultimate day of the Stour Valley Path enjoys a mixture of old railway tracks and meadow paths past the historic market town of Sudbury. Here the route detours away from the river due to a lack of rights of way and instead takes in the gentle rolling hills around the hamlets of Middleton, Great Henny and Lamarsh before arriving in the small village of Bures. It's possible to break the walk down further here thanks to regular train services to Marks Tey and Sudbury but for those continuing to Nayland there's several miles of more riverside and countryside walking to enjoy before resting the legs and preparing for the final day of the trail.

Stage 3: Long Melford to Nayland
Distance: 26.9km / 16.7 Miles

From Long Melford high street, head south to the village library just opposite the George and Dragon Pub. The path follows the alley with a wavy wall on the right past a small graveyard and along a straight alley to the road. Turn right to the open playing field and keep along the left hand edge to the far corner. Join the path directly ahead and follow it as it curves round to the left along the boundary to the football ground and up to a gate. Head through the gate into the open grazing field and follow the faint path directly ahead past the line of bushes and trees and to the far side where the path arrives near an old overflow weir. Head over to the banks of the Stour and turn left, heading over the concrete weir and along the river to a footbridge. Cross the bridge past Liston weir until you reach the road turn right, keeping an eye out for a footpath/driveway on the left after about 70m.

Long Melford

Long Melford is a stunning historic village with two stately homes and dozens of listed timber framed houses. The origins of the village date back to Roman times where a large settlement built up by the River Stour which was navigable at this time providing trade links around the empire. From the medieval period onward it became a prosperous wool town, similar to that of Lavenham and has maintained its historic architecture and wide high street.

Turn left down the driveway briefly and turn left along the footpath which skirts the grounds to the property and along several field edges. After a couple of fields the path follows a hedge line up to the road. Turn left and follow the lane south to the junction and bear left again. This follows a short section of a fairly busy road so take care and after 450 the road bends to the left so it's worth crossing at some point and using the bank on the opposite side. Just before the road bridge turn right along the line of the old Sudbury to Melford Railway and follow it for 1.4km to an information board detailing the Gainsborough Trail at a junction of several paths. Bear left here along a track and follow it up to the minor road. Keep left here passing Brundon Mill and a series of cottages and to the entrance to Brundon Hall. Here the path turns right along the edge of the hall grounds with a small pond in the trees on the right and leads up to a gate. Head through the gate and along the path between the paddocks eventually up to the footbridge leading into open water meadow.

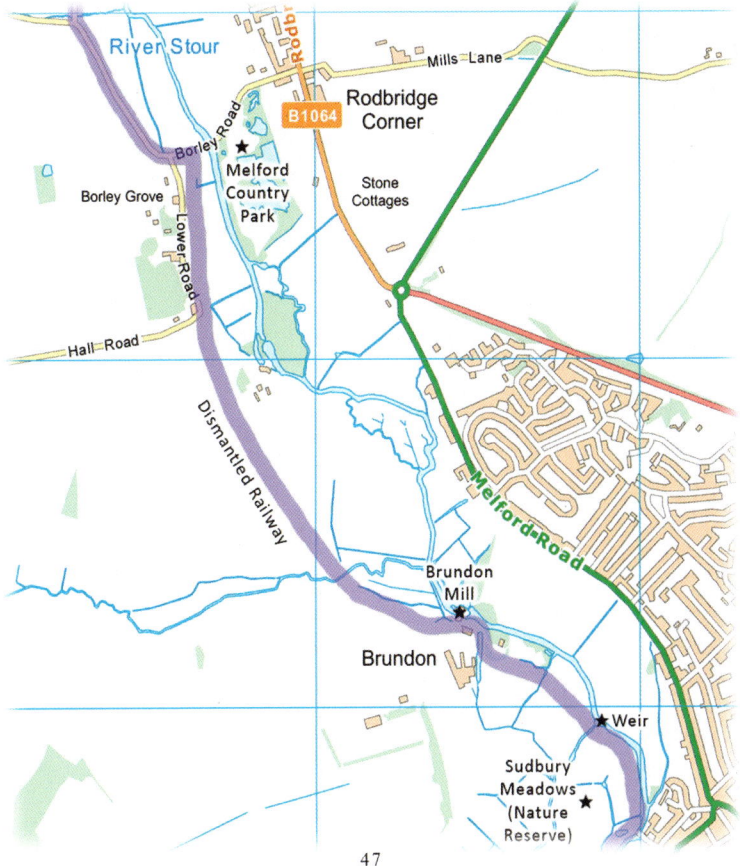

Brundon Mill

Brundon Mill is a former watermill now converted into a dwelling. It dates to the 18th Century and has been given the protection of a Grade II listing.

Brundon Mill

Cross the field directly ahead, passing a derelict pillbox, to a footbridge by a weir. Continue through the gates into the next field and follow the faint path along the river on the left until you reach the gate on the other side close to a footbridge. Do not cross the footbridge, instead stick to the riverbank path round past a bridge by The Croft and along the river until you reach the Mill Hotel. At the corner of the Mill Hotel a gate leads into the open meadow where a faint path crosses the grass to the left. Halfway along the meadow the path crosses a shallow ditch and then continues up to the trees where there is a footbridge just on the left hand side. Cross the river via the footbridge and turn left following a faint path south through the meadow and up to a gate by an old pump-house.

Sudbury Water Meadows

Sudbury Water Meadows is a lovely local nature reserve offering the perfect place to sit and watch kingfishers dart in and out of the gently flowing waters or ducks dabbling in the pool below the Mill Hotel. The meadows form part of a larger area of open access land which is grazed by cattle throughout the spring and summer months with the Stour Valley Path exploring much of this lovely area.

Sudbury Water Meadows

St Peter's Church, Sudbury

Sudbury

Sudbury is a large historic market town with origins dating back to Saxon times. The town grew more prosperous in the late medieval period thanks to local textile business which funded many of the wealthy buildings and churches in the town. Sudbury was also home to one of the most famous painters in the 18th Century; Thomas Gainsborough. Gainsborough is now well known for his landscape paintings of the local area and became an inspiration for John Constable with many of their paintings in London galleries. Walkers who have time and an interest in art should visit the Gainsborough Museum set within Thomas Gainsborough's childhood house and displays his paintings.

The Mill Hotel

The Mill Hotel is a former Corn Mill which dates to the 17th Century with documentation of a building on this site since the Domesday Book. Now used as a restaurant and hotel, the building is protected with a Grade II listing.

The Mill Hotel

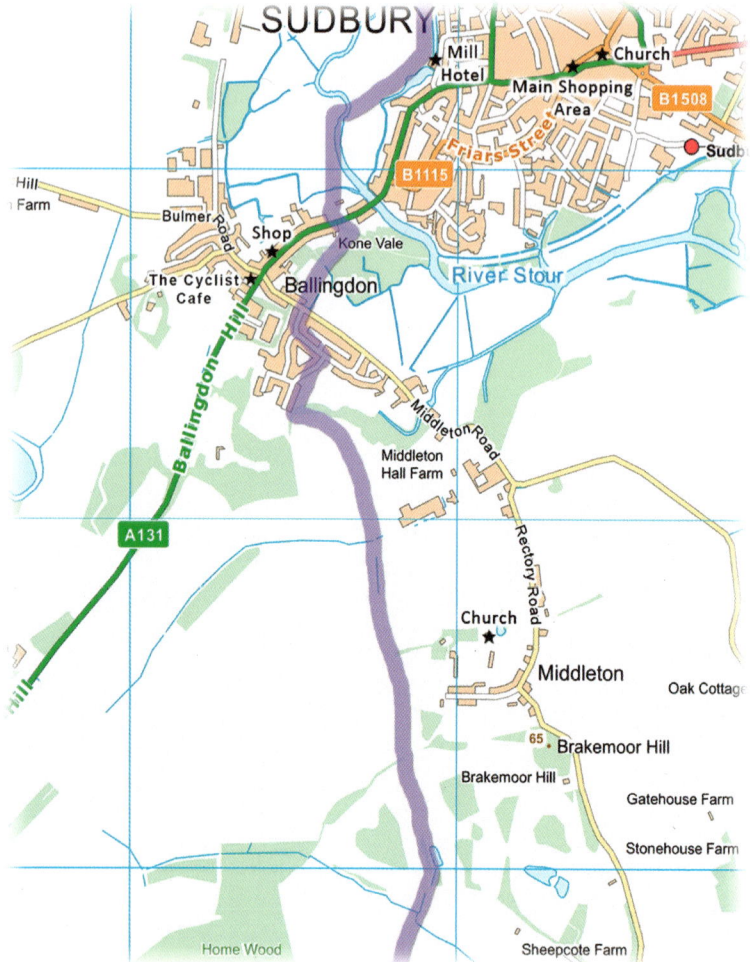

Head through the gate and continue along the tarmac ahead almost up to the road but just before it there is a path on the right leading up to the railway line once again. Once on the line turn left over the railway bridge and take the first path on the right shortly ahead. The path passes through some fields surrounded by woodland and eventually arrives at Middleton road. Head down Meadow View Road opposite and follow it round to the left and up to a play park just over to the right along Pinecroft Rise. Turn right along Pinecroft Rise and at the end of the play park on the left there is a footpath leading into the trees and along the back of a line of houses. The path then turns left and climbs to the top of a small escarpment and then along a straight avenue of bushes to an open field.

Cross the field and follow the edge of the bushes until you reach the farm track just ahead. Continue straight, heading south along the track keeping the field to the right and hedge/tree line to the left as you gently ascend. After about 600m the path crosses a track going left to right and continues straight ahead on a gentle descent along the right hand side of some trees and then alongside a small area of woodland to an open field. Turn right and just ahead at the corner the path crosses the boundary on the right into the adjacent field and turns left (south). Approximately 600m along the edge of the field the path crosses the boundary on the left and turns right along the edge of the field to the south again. After about 160m at the gentle curve of the corner of the field the path branches to the right along another field edge and after following the edge of a second field the path passes through a paddock just by Thorncroft Farm. The route leaves the paddock and joins a straight path along the edge of a field and property to reach the lane close to Great Henny Church.

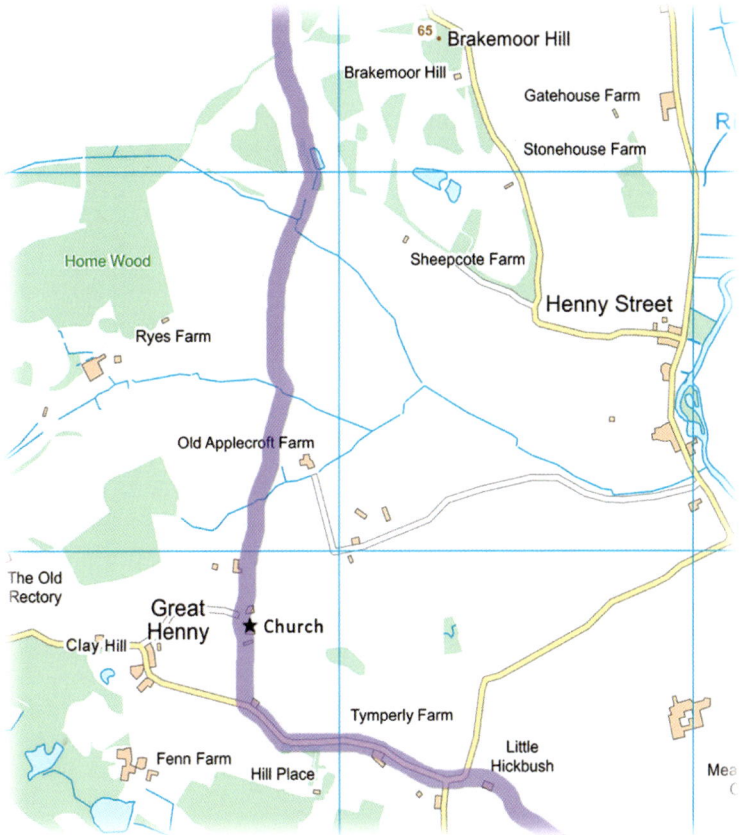

St Mary's Church, Great Henny

Great Henny Church, dedicated to St Mary, is a Grade II* listed building dating to the late 11th or early 12th Century. The church was extended and altered in the 14th and 16th Century and is registered as a small place of pilgrimage.

St Mary's Church, Great Henny

Head through the church yard, past the church and out along the access track to the south until you reach the road and turn left. The road is followed for 700m to the second turning on the right signposted to 'Hickbush Only'. Follow this narrow lane gently round past a house and along the fields until you reach the next house about 350m further along. Just before the house turn left along a footpath between the field and garden which is a little uneven and steep in places until you reach a path which turns right and crosses the field under the pylons. On the other side of the field the path crosses a footbridge and turns right along paddocks to a farm. The track passes through the farm and along the driveway to the south. After about 200m keep an eye out for the continuation of the footpath through a gate on the right as the right of way does not stick to the driveway. Turn right through the gate and follow a pathless section south through the grazing field and up the hill to which on the far southern side there is a gate leading onto the road.

At the road turn left and follow it for just over 250m to a footpath on the right. Turn right and follow the fence lined path as it gently curves round to the left and descends down to the road close to the spired church in Lamarsh. Turn right and follow the road into Lamarsh where it turns sharply to the left and continues to the Lamarsh Lion. Just 50m past the Lion pub the Stour Valley Path bears left along a track and past several houses to reach the railway line. Take care crossing the line and head into the field opposite with the River Stour just down to the left by a pillbox. Follow the edge of the grazing field to the far side where the path joins a track and bears right to head south east along the field edge eventually arriving close to the village of Bures. Just before a farm the path bears left and shortly arrives at the road.

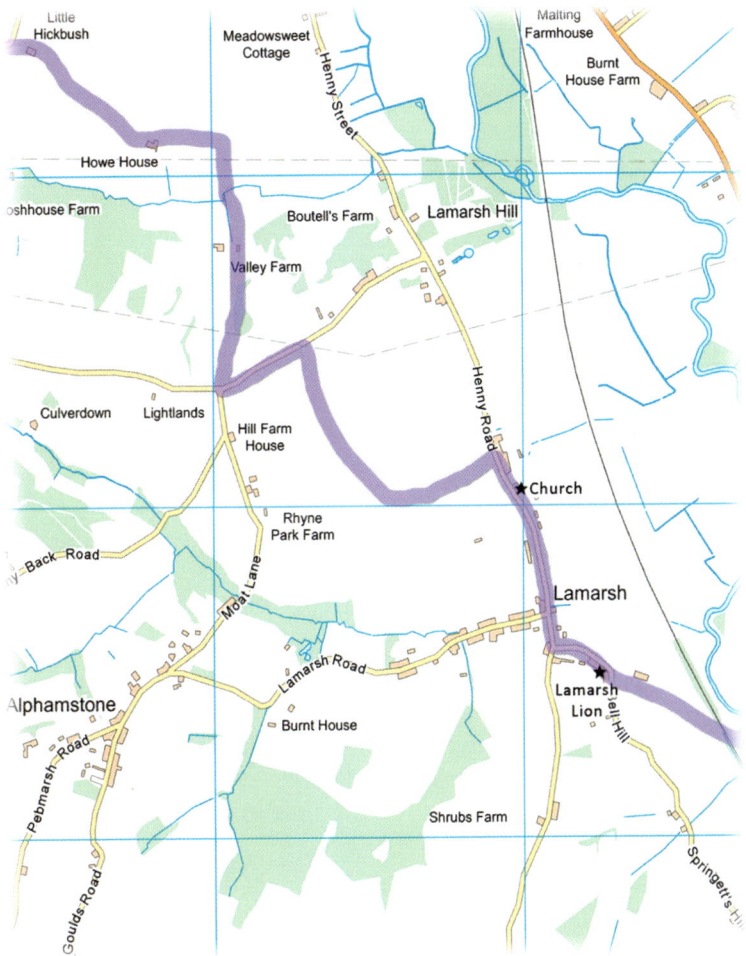

Holy Innocents, Lamarsh

Lamarsh has a stunning Grade I listed spired church dedicated to the Holy Innocents. This dedication is incredibly rare, being one of only 5 churches in England to have it. The church was built in the mid 12th Century with alterations in the 14th Century and restorations in 1869.

Lamarsh Church

Bures

Bures is a lovely small village that is actually made up of two parishes, Bures Hamlet on the Essex side of the River Stour and Bures St Mary on the Suffolk side. There's a village pub, shop and deli as well as the stunning Grade I listed church of St Mary dating to the 14th Century. Bures is a perfect place to break the walk down further thanks to excellent public transport links back to Sudbury and onto Marks Tey or stay at the local B&B.

River Stour at Bures

Turn left along the road through Bures and over the River Stour to the parish church. Turn right just after the church and follow the road round a series of bends to a footpath on the right just after the Community Centre. Follow the path around the field edge and up to the track and turn right to the split just ahead. Bear left towards Bures Mill, keeping right just before the entrance way which leads to a footbridge over the river to grazing fields on the other side. Turn left crossing the field towards a stile and continue in a straight line through several other fields until you reach the trackway by a large house. Cross the track and follow the path opposite along the field edge to the other side. Here the path heads through the boundary and into the open field where it crosses diagonally to the right towards a small clump of trees. Cross over the track and follow the path opposite along the trees and across the field to the grazing pasture. Head into the grazing field and turn right to gently ascend up to a trackway on the other side of the fence. Ignore the track left and right and instead continue straight ahead towards a gate which then joins a path along a fence to the east. The path descends down to woodland and through the trees to the church yard and then arrives at the road.

Bures Mill

Bures Mill is a lovely watermill passed as you leave the nearby village. The mill dates to either the 18th or 19th Century and given a Grade II listing.

Bures Mill

St Andrew, Wormingford

Wormingford is a tiny hamlet with a stunning church showing hints of its Norman origins. Dedicated to St Andrew, the church has been given the protection of a Grade I listing thanks to its significant historic and architectural interest.

Turn left along the lane and turn right down a track at the end of the church yard. At the end of the track the path enters an open field and follows the field edge directly ahead and round to the left. The path gently curves round to the right and joins a tree lined path for 200m to a trackway. Ignore the track leading round to the right towards the farm and instead continue east (directly ahead) under the telegraph lines and cross the field boundary ahead into the grazing field. Cross the field and then through the field boundary just ahead. Once on the other side follow the path diagonally to the right (south east) up to a trackway called Garnons Chase. Turn left and follow Garnons Chase for just over 600m to a footpath on the right through some trees and along a field edge by some small ponds. The path bears left once you reach the woodland ahead and continues about 150m before turning left along the edge of paddocks and eventually arriving at the road north of Malting Farm.

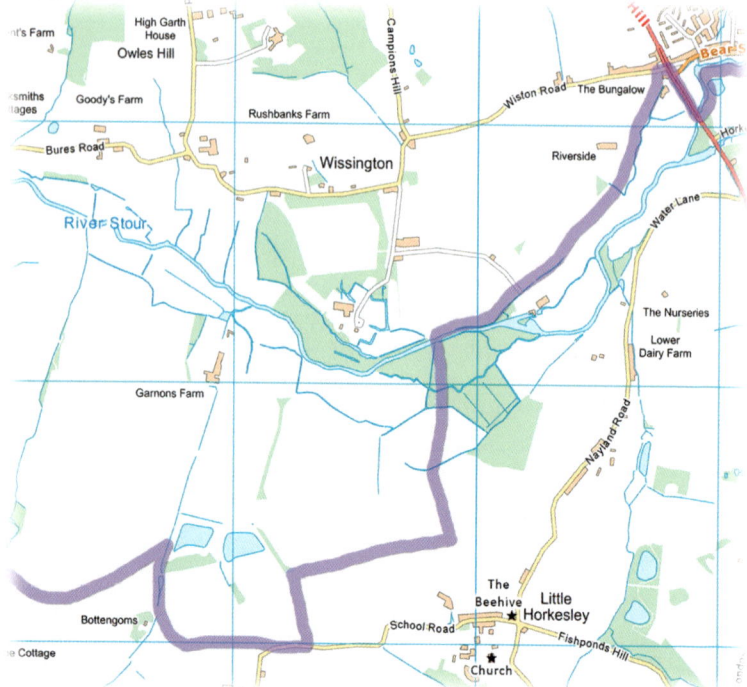

Turn left and follow the lane for just 150m to a footpath on the left which leads along the field edge and at the far side joins a faint track. Turn right and follow the track along the field edge where you will then cross School Lane and follow the field edge on the other side. After 260m along the field edge turn left to head north through the middle of the field, cross the boundary and pass through the middle of the next fields to arrive at woodland. Follow the path through the wood and then the plantation to a footbridge over the River Stour. Turn right and follow the path parallel to the river on the right which leads to the driveway for Wiston Mill. Head over the driveway and follow the field edge path directly ahead which enters grazing marsh after 570m. Follow the path along the right hand edge of the grazing marshes until you reach the road in Nayland. Once at the road turn right up to the main road just ahead and cross carefully. Turn right to follow the edge of the green, keeping the main road on the right until you cross the River Stour just ahead. Take the riverside path on the left which follows the southern side of the River Stour, passing a lovely wildlife pond and curving round to a weir on the opposite bank to some riverside properties. Continue past the weir and stick to the path close to the river which arrives at the road close to the Anchor Inn. Turn left past the Anchor Inn and into the village centre of Nayland.

The final day of the Stour Valley Path begins in the small riverside village of Nayland and traverses along the entire length of the Dedham Vale area of outstanding natural beauty to end by the coast at Cattawade. The beautiful villages of Stoke by Nayland and Stratford St Mary offer a choice of pubs to enjoy lunch at before the traverse along the riverbank by Dedham and Flatford. The countryside around Flatford is always bustling with tourists during the summer months thanks to its lovely scenery, iconic Mill and nearby cottage that was painted by John Constable. This has led the area to be known as Constable Country.

Stage 4: Nayland to Cattawade
Distance: 21.2km / 13.17 Miles

From the centre of Nayland, follow the road north to a sharp bend with a signpost point left for Colchester and the A134, and right for Stoke, Ipswich and the B1087. Turn right along the road signposted to Stoke and take the first road (Gravel Hill) on the left just ahead. The road gently curves round to the right and then follows a straight section for about 800m to a bend round to the right. Here the path continues straight ahead along the line of trees to the north. After 350m the path crosses a stream and joins the edge of the field, still heading north. At a sharp corner of the field boundary the path bears right across the open field to head north through a hedge line on the other side and across a second field to join a track. At the track turn right and follow it for 550m to rejoin the road. Keep left and follow the road for just 120m to a track branching off to the right. Follow the track past Poplars Farmhouse B&B and then at the split just beyond keep left. This track leads towards Stoke by Nayland and arrives at the road opposite the stunning parish church.

Nayland

Nayland is a lovely small village with an outstanding pub, small shop and local butchers. There's a local B&B for an overnight stay with another just out of the village on the way to Stoke by Nayland. Alternatively there are bus links into Sudbury but these tend to stop from mid afternoon so a taxi later in the day would be more suitable. The lovely Grade I listed church of St James sits in the village centre and dates to the 14th Century and crowned with a classic spire.

Court Knoll, Nayland

Court Knoll is a large earthwork on the south side of Nayland just set back from the River Stour. It's initial presentation appears like a ringwork or motte & bailey castle but excavations in 2016 revealed what appeared to be the remains of an early medieval chapel. To this day archaeologists are still uncertain of the earthworks origin.

Court Knoll

St Mary, Stoke by Nayland

The cathedral-like church in Stoke by Nayland is a well known landmark in the surrounding countryside, and can be seen from miles around as the west tower climbs to a height of 120ft. Dedicated to St Mary and built in the 15th Century, the church replaced an older building on the site which was recorded in the Domesday Book of 1085, the only remnant being the Late Norman Piscina in the north chapel.

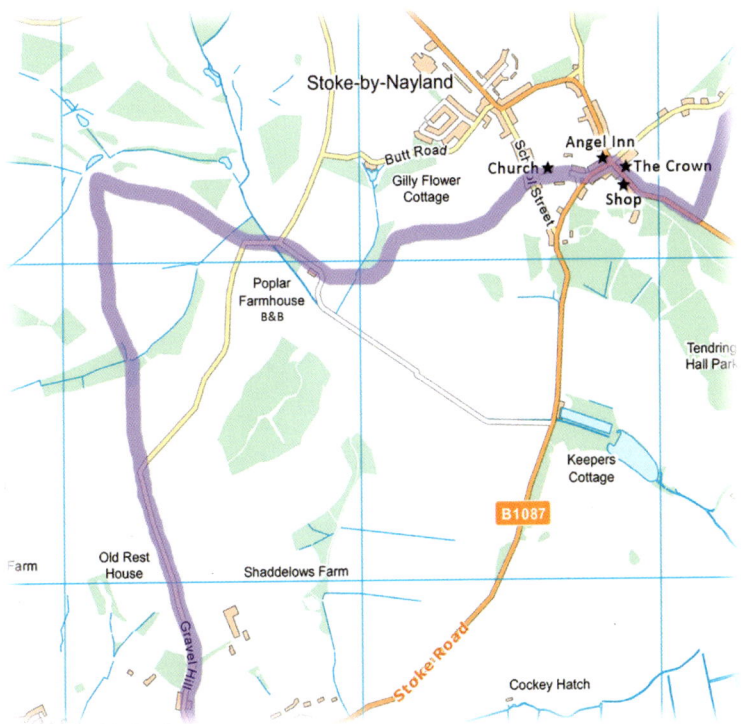

Cross the road and follow the path just to the right of the church along a wall and up to a triangle of grass. Keep left and follow the road up to the junction by the Angel Inn and turn right past the Crown and small village shop to join the roadside grassy path on the left. This is followed just a short way to a gate where the path turns away from the road and along the left hand edge of the field and at the far corner turns round to the right along the edge and into a small clump of trees. The path leaves the trees along a diagonal path across the field to join another path at the other side and turns right. After 320m the path joins a track, bear left and follow the track past farm buildings and then left over the River Box. Follow the track straight ahead around a very gentle s-bend and up to the split 100m ahead. Turn right and almost straight away there is a gate and path on the left leading along the edge of the field to the east. At the corner of the field the path enters the edge of a small wood and then along the edge of the field to arrive at a track. Follow the track opposite to continue east until you reach the road and turn right. After just 20m the Stour Valley Path turns left along a track, past a small wood and then across an open field to a sharp bend left leading past a farm building and house.

Countryside around Stoke by Nayland

Just over 200m past the house there is a junction, turn right here and follow the track for about 350m to a split just after a sharp bend. Turn left following the tree lined track east and then gently round to the right to head south along a path between trees. Follow this path for a little over 1.2km as it takes a series of sharp bends as it works its way south to eventually join the road. Turn left and briefly follow the road to the first track on the right which heads south along hedge lines. Follow the hedge lined track until you reach the open field at the end where the track turns right and then sharply left just ahead. The path follows the edge of the field and after about 600m arrives at a narrow stream and footbridge. Cross the footbridge and follow the path through the trees and over the River Stour and past the building just on the right. At the sharp bend just ahead turn left to take a path across the field in a straight line and once at the field edge cross the next field to join a track on the other side.

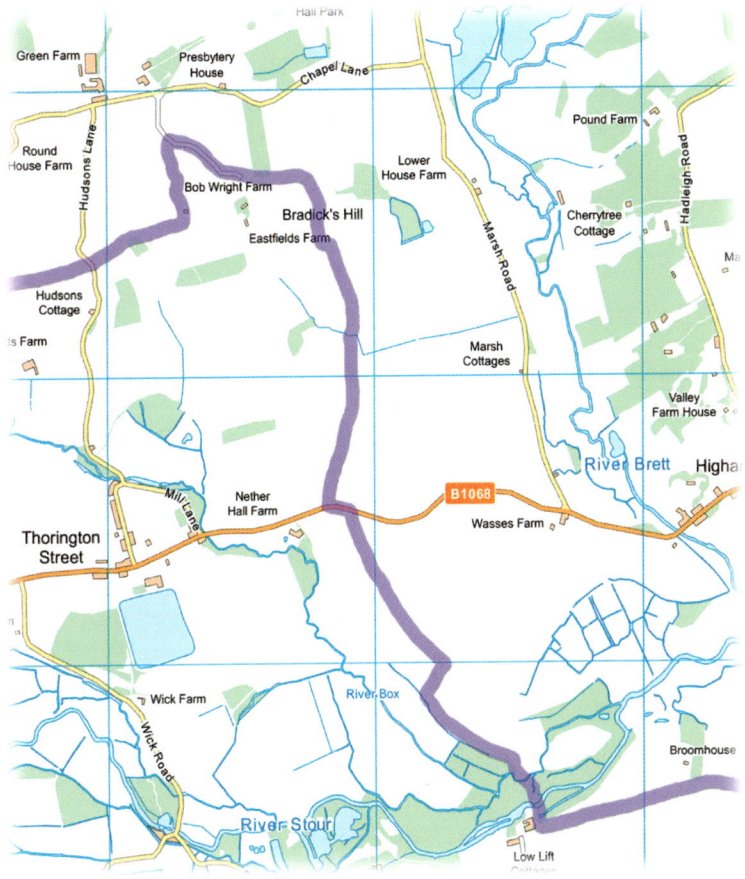

At the sharp bend in the track just 30m ahead you need to enter the field directly in front. Follow the field edge to the left and then round to the right to head east. Shortly you may notice a lovely lake over to the left which is a haven for wildlife and the path skirts along the south side of it. Once at the end of the lake the path heads off the well defined track that developed and into the trees on the left to join the bank of the River Stour. Follow it right, through the riverside woodland until you reach a gate where the path then crosses the open field diagonally to the right and arrives at a footbridge.

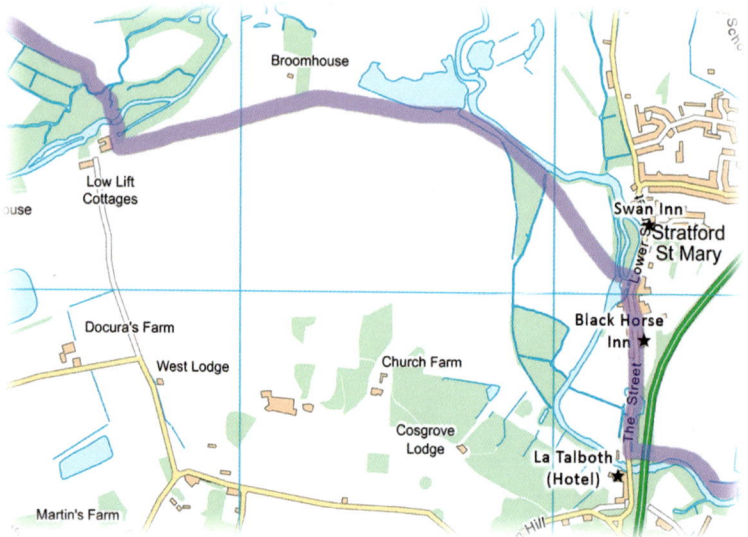

Cross the footbridge over the River Stour and continue in a straight line to the road only a few metres ahead. Turn right to follow the road through Stratford St Mary and after 200m passes the Black Horse Inn. Continue a further 320m south along the road until you reach a track on the left which passes through a gate and under the busy A12. As you emerge on the other side of the A12 the path continues straight ahead into the grazing field and follows the meandering north bank of the River Stour. The riverbank path is followed for a little over 1.6km and arrives at the road just north of Dedham with an optional detour into the village centre for refreshments. On the opposite side of the road the path re-enters the grazing fields, still on the north side of the river, and continues for 300m to the first tree line/old field boundary. Shortly after the line of trees the path actually splits, it's here you need to keep left which follows a straight line across the field to the east. The path arrives at a gate and onto a straight path between trees. After 330m the path arrives at a junction where you need to turn right, gently curving round to a footbridge.

Dedham Vale

Dedham Vale is an area of outstanding natural beauty that covers the lower part of the Stour Valley and much of the Stour Estuary, covering an area of 90 square kilometres. The whole area was made famous thanks to the legendary romantic painter John Constable with his best works on show at the Victoria and Albert Museum in London. Some of his most famous works include that of Flatford Mill and Willy Lott's Cottage which are both passed directly along the route.

The River Stour at Dedham

Boat trips along he River Stour at Flatford

Flatford Mill & Willy Lott's Cottage

Flatford Mill is a stunning Grade I listed watermill dating to 1733. The mill is in the care of the National Trust and currently used as a field studies centre. Opposite the mill is Willy Lott's Cottage dating to the late 16th Century. This is also protected as a Grade I listed building due to its significance in the works of John Constable.

Flatford Mill

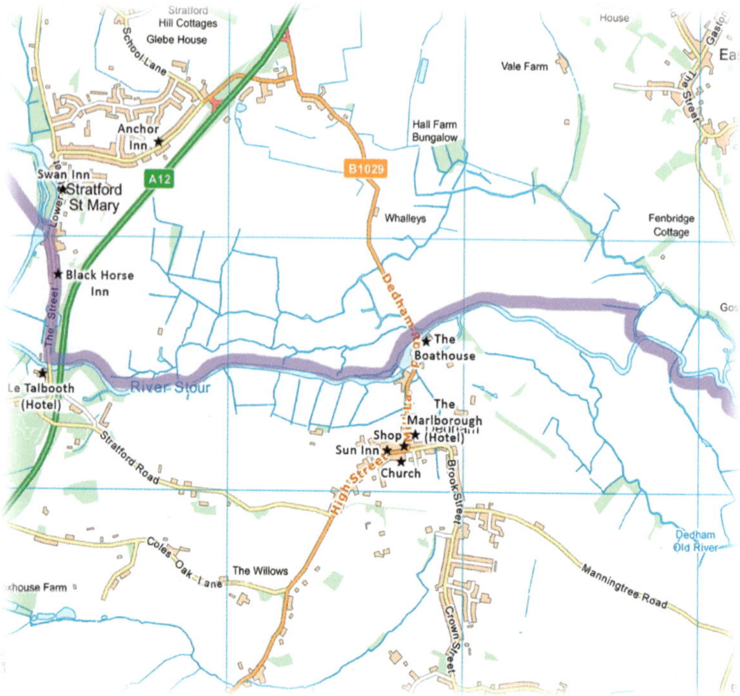

Willy Lott's Cottage

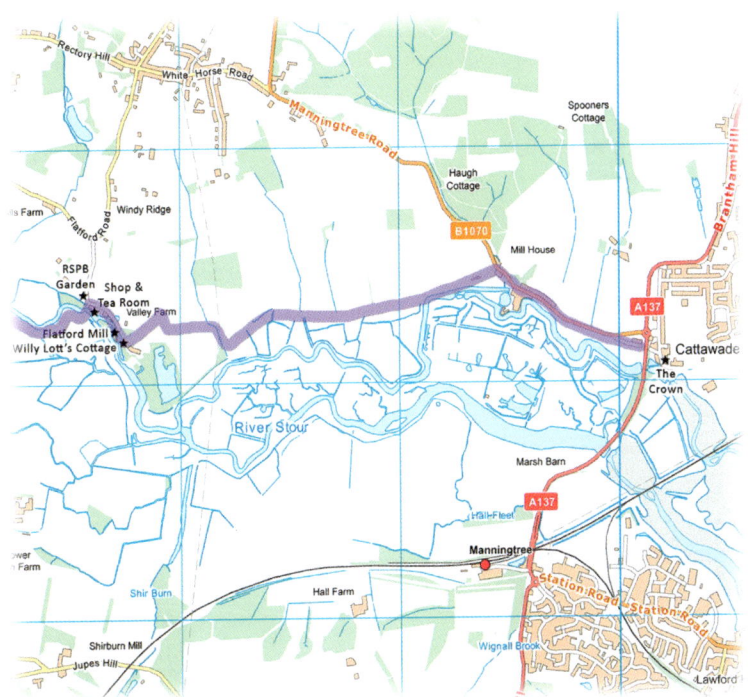

Cross the footbridge onto the south side of the River Stour and turn left, following the riverbank through grazing fields for 1.1km to Flatford Bridge. Cross the bridge to the junction ahead and turn right past the small National Trust shop and tea room. The lane shortly arrives at Flatford Mill and one of the most iconic scenes in the whole of Dedham Vale AONB. Follow the track past Willy Lott's Cottage where it splits and keep left, heading along the straight path. After 170m, just before the gate, follow the path round to the right. 80m along this path it bends sharply left and heads east to arrive just before a large metal pylon. Head into the field and turn right under the pylon and along the field edge to another gate. Pass through this gate into the field and turn left, following the path along the edge of the marsh to the east. The path keeps close to the field edge with vast open nature reserve to the south. After 1.1km the path crosses to the other side of the field boundary on the left and continues east along the field edge to the road. Turn right to follow the road south east past a small industrial estate and eventually to a fork in the road which is signposted to a picnic site. Take the right hand road towards the picnic site and after 120m you will arrive at the edge of Cattawade with the River Stour just over to the right, officially marking the end of the trail.

For those with a little extra time and energy, at the corner of the car park there is a path up to the main road. Cross the main road carefully and head down the lane opposite towards The Crown pub. Just beyond the pub on the right is the start of the Stour Estuary, which at low tide is alive with all types of wading birds and wildlife. Although right near the official end of the trail, this is the point where the River Stour becomes the Stour Estuary, with water levels managed by the nearby sluice. To reach the nearby train station simply follow the main road (A137) south over the River Stour and along the edge of the estuary for 1.2km to the railway line with the station just over to the right providing regular links into Colchester and Ipswich.

Cattawade Picnic Site

Appendix
Useful Information

General:
Long Distance Walkers Association
www.ldwa.org.uk

National Rail Enquiries
www.nationalrail.co.uk

Newmarket:
Rutland Arms Hotel
www.therutlandarms.co.uk
01638 664 251

Kings Newmarket (Hotel)
www.kingsnewmarket.co.uk
01638 660 668

White Hart (Hotel)
www.whitehartnewmarket.co.uk
01638 663 051

The Jockey Club Rooms
www.jockeyclubrooms.co.uk
01638 663 101

The Cambridgeshire B&B
www.thecambridgeshire.co.uk
01638 601 829

Best Western Heath Court Hotel
www.heathcourthotel.com
01638 667 171

Premier Inn Newmarket
www.premierinn.com
0333 321 9232

The Waggon & Horses
www.thewaggonpub.com
01638 560 265

Cortado Espresso Bar
www.cortadoespressobar.com
07740 421 064

Nancy's Tea Shop
www.nancysteashop.co.uk
01638 667 064

Hmmburger
www.hmmburger.co.uk
01638 668 432

Wildwood
www.wildwoodrestaurants.co.uk
01638 667 584

The Golden Lion
www.jdwetherspoon.com
01638 672 040

Deep Blue Restaurant
www.deepbluerestaurants.com
01638 662 898

Street Cafe
High Street. Newmarket
01638 428 099

Stetchworth:
Cross Green B&B
www.crossgreenbandb.co.uk
01638 508 322

The Old Mill, Stetchworth
www.theoldmill.info
01638 507 839

Marquis of Granby
01638 508 383

Thurlow:
The Cock Inn
www.thethurlowcock.co.uk
01440 783 224

Kedington:
The Barnardiston Arms
www.the-barnardiston-arms.edan.io
01440 703 145

Appendix
Useful Information

Stoke by Clare:
Pickwick House B&B
www.pickwick-house-bed-breakfast.suffolk-hotels.co.uk
01787 278 707

The Lion
www.thelionstokebyclare.com
01787 277 571

Clare:
Cobbles B&B
www.cobblesclare.co.uk
01787 277 539

The Bell Hotel
www.thebellhotelclare.co.uk
01787 277 741

Ship Stores B&B
www.ship-stores.co.uk
01787 277 834

The Swan
01787 278 280

The Globe Pub
01787 278 122

Cafe Clare
www.cafe-clare.co.uk
01787 278 148

Number One Deli
www.numberonedeli.co.uk
01787 278 932

Tuckermans Sandwich Shop
www.tuckermans.co.uk
01787 278 351

Platform One Cafe
01787 277 850

Coop Food
Market Hill, Clare

Cavendish:
Five Bells
01787 280 070

The George Hotel
www.thecavendishgeorge.co.uk
01787 280 248

The Bull
01787 280 245

Tea on the Green
www.teaonthegreencavendish.co.uk
07757 355 872

Duck or Grouse Community Shop
01787 282 371

Glemsford:
Greyhound Cottage B&B
www.greyhoundcottage.com
01787 281 897

Black Lion
01787 280 684

Angel Inn
01787 281 559

Hunts Hill Store
01787 280 270

Rumbles Chip Shop
www.rumbles-chip-shop.edan.io
01787 280 918

Long Melford:
The Black Lion Hotel
www.theblacklionlongmelford.com
01787 312 356

The Swan
www.longmelfordswan.co.uk
01787 468 653

The Mill B&B
www.themill-longmelford.com
01787 378 035

Appendix
Useful Information

The Crown Inn
www.thecrownhotelmelford.co.uk
01787 377 666

The Bull Hotel
www.greeneking-pubs.co.uk
01787 378 494

The George & Dragon Hotel
www.thegeorgeanddragonhotel.com
01787 371 285

Denmark House B&B
www.denmarkhousebb.co.uk
01787 378 798

St Catherine's Cottage B&B
Liston Lane, Long Melford
07899 696 491

Holgate B&B
01787 882 170

The Cock & Bell
www.greeneking-pubs.co.uk
01787 379 807

Scutchers Restaurant
www.scutchers.com
01787 310 200

The Olive Tree Tearooms
01787 371 060

Long Melford Tea Room
01787 881 361

Melford Valley Tandoori
www.melfordvalley.com
01787 310 079

Chips 'n' Chopstix
www.chips-n-chopstix.business.site
01787 378 776

Sudbury:
The Mill Hotel
www.themillhotelsudbury.co.uk
01787 375 544

The Angel, Sudbury
www.angelpubsudbury.co.uk
01787 204 650

The Bay Horse Inn
www.bayhorsesudbury.co.uk
01787 377 450

Mill House B&B
www.millhouse-sudbury.co.uk
01787 882 966

Hill Lodge Hotel
www.hilllodgehotel.co.uk
01787 377 568

North Street Tavern
01787 828 018

Grover & Allen
www.jdwetherspoon.co.uk
01787 467 660

The White Horse
www.whitehorsesudbury.co.uk
01787 374 321

Twenteaone Cafe
www.twenteaone.co.uk
01787 312 783

Starburger Cafe
North Street, Sudbury
01787 379 413

Joe's Sandwich Shop
North Street, Sudbury
01787 883 393

Chill-In Cafe & Bistro
Old Market Square, Sudbury
01787 376 488

Appendix
Useful Information

Prado Lounge
www.thelounges.co.uk
01787 313 634

The Wagon Gastropub
www.thewagonsudbury.co.uk
01787 312 147

Lydia Turkish Kitchen
www.lydiakitchen.co.uk
01787 466 781

Painters Cafe
Gainsborough Street, Sudbury
07380 988 224

The Bridge Project Tea Room
www.thebridgeproject.co.uk
01787 313 691

Huffers Cafe
www.huffers-of-sudbury.business.site
01787 881 919

The Strawberry Teapot
www.thestrawberryteapot.co.uk
01787 881 999

A Slice of New York (Pizzaria)
www.asliceofnewyork.co.uk
01787 372 512

The Secret Garden Cafe
www.tsguk.net
01787 312 301

Alaz Turkish Cuisine
www.alazrestaurant.co.uk
01787 370 001

The Cyclist Cafe
www.cyclistsudbury.co.uk
07842 783 473

Lamarsh:
The Lamarsh Lion
www.lamarshlion.co.uk
01787 227 007

Bures:
Old Manse B&B
07875 435 369

Eight Bells Pub
Colchester Road, Bures
01787 227 354

Village Deli
Bridge Street, Bures
01787 228 032

Wormingford:
The Crown at Wormingford
www.thecrownwormingford.co.uk
01787 227 464

Nayland:
Stourbank Cottage
Bear Street, Nayland
01206 262 065

Poplars Farmhouse B&B
www.poplarsfarmhouse.com
01206 265 101

Anchor Inn
www.anchornayland.co.uk
01206 262 313

Stoke by Nayland:
The Angel Inn
www.angelinnsuffolk.co.uk
01206 263 245

The Crown Inn
www.crowninn.net
01206 262 001

Stratford St Mary:
The Anchor Inn
www.anchor-st-mary.edan.io
01206 322 143

The Swan Inn
www.stratfordswan.com
01206 321 244

Appendix
Useful Information

Black Horse Inn
Lower Street, Stratford St Mary
01206 321 682

Le Talbooth Hotel & Restaurant
www.milsomhotels.com
01206 323 150

Dedham:
The Sun Inn Hotel
www.thesuninndedham.com
01206 323 351

The Marlborough Hotel
www.themarlboroughdedham.co.uk
01206 323 250

Dedham Hall
www.dedhamhall.co.uk
01206 323 027

The Boathouse
www.dedhamboathouse.com
01206 323 153

Old Bakery Cafe
www.oldbakerycafe.co.uk
01206 619 106

Flatford:
National Trust Tea Room
www.nationaltrust.org.uk

Cattawade:
Crown at Cattawade
www.cattawadecrown.co.uk
01206 392 800

The Ark Bar & Restaurant
Cattawade Street, Cattawade
01206 396 777

Notes

Printed in Great Britain
by Amazon